Collins English Library

Series editors: K R Cripwell and ~~~~~~

A library of graded r .... tant
native readers. The ....
idiom and sentence l ....
in *A Teacher's Guide* ....
level. Level 1 has a b ....
words, 3: 1000 words,
which are asterisked a

Five Ghost Stories* *Viola Huggins*
Three English Kings *from Shakespeare*
An American Tragedy *Theodore Dreiser*
Six American Stories* *N Wymer*
Emma and I *Sheila Hocken*
Little Women *Louisa M Alcott*
The Picture of Dorian Gray* *Oscar Wilde*
Maimunah *David Hill*
Marilyn Monroe *Peter Dainty*
Bruce Springsteen *Toni Murphy*
Is That It? *Bob Geldof*
Short Stories *Oscar Wilde*
A Room with a View *E M Forster*
The Importance of Being Ernest *Oscar Wilde*
The Lost World *Sir Arthur Conan Doyle*
Arab Folk Tales *Helen Thomson*
Computers: From Beads to Bytes *Peter Dewar*

Level Four

The White South *Hammond Innes*
A Christmas Carol *Charles Dickens*
King Solomon's Mines* *H Rider Haggard*
Jane Eyre *Charlotte Brontë*
Pride and Prejudice *Jane Austen*
Dr Jekyll and Mr Hyde* *R L Stevenson*
Huckleberry Finn *Mark Twain*
Landslide *Desmond Bagley*
Nothing is the Number When You Die *Joan Fleming*
The African Child *Camara Laye*
The Lovely Lady and other Stories *D H Lawrence*
Airport International *Brian Moynahan*
The Secret Sharer and other Sea Stories *Joseph Conrad*
Death in Vienna? *K E Rowlands*
Hostage Tower* *Alistair MacLean*
The Potter's Wheel *Chukwuemeka Ike*
Tina Turner *Stephen Rabley*
Campbell's Kingdom *Hammond Innes*

Level Five

The Guns of Navarone *Alistair MacLean*
Geordie *David Walker*
Wuthering Heights *Emily Brontë*
Where Eagles Dare *Alistair MacLean*
Wreck of the Mary Deare *Hammond Innes*
I Know My Love *Catherine Gaskin*
Among the Elephants *Iain and Oria Douglas-Hamilton*
The Mayor of Casterbridge *Thomas Hardy*
Sense and Sensibility *Jane Austen*
The Eagle has Landed *Jack Higgins*
Middlemarch *George Eliot*
Victory *Joseph Conrad*
Experiences of Terror* *Roland John*
Japan: Islands in the Mist *Peter Milward*

Level Six

Doctor Zhivago *Boris Pasternak*
The Glory Boys *Gerald Seymour*
In the Shadow of Man *Jane Goodall*
Harry's Game *Gerald Seymour*
House of a Thousand Lanterns *Victoria Holt*
Hard Times *Charles Dickens*
Sons and Lovers *D H Lawrence*
The Dark Frontier *Eric Ambler*
Vanity Fair *William Thackeray*
Inspector Ghote Breaks an Egg *H R F Keating*

Collins English Library Level 3

THREE ENGLISH KINGS
FROM SHAKESPEARE

Contents

Simplified and retold by Margery Morris

COLLINS
E·L·T

© Margery Morris 1981

Published in Great Britain by
William Collins Sons and Co Ltd
Glasgow G4 0NB

Printed by Martin's of Berwick

First published in Collins English Library, 1981
Reprinted: 1983, 1985, 1987, 1989, 1990

ISBN 0 00 370128 X

Illustrations by Willie Rodger

We are grateful to Reg Wilson Photography for permission to
reproduce the photograph which appears on the cover.

King Richard the Second

God's Chosen King

Five hundred years ago, people believed that a king was chosen by God. Fighting against a king, or killing him, was the worst crime. Everybody knew this, but not everybody remembered it when they were angry.

King Richard the Second was a young man. His uncle, John of Gaunt, tried to teach and help him, but Richard did not often listen to the old man.

One day, John of Gaunt told Richard that two of the lords were quarrelling. One was Thomas Mowbray, Duke of Norfolk. The other was Henry Bolingbroke, Earl of Hereford. Bolingbroke was John of Gaunt's son, and the king's cousin.

"Bring them to me," said Richard. "I will decide."

Bolingbroke and Mowbray were brought to the king. Both men were very angry, but they bent low in front of him.

Bolingbroke said, "My loving lord."

"Happiness," said Mowbray, "I hope you'll be happy all your life."

"Thank you," said Richard. "Cousin Boling-broke, why do you argue with Mowbray?"

Bolingbroke said, "There have been many plans to kill you, my lord, and he is behind them all. You gave him money to pay your soldiers, and he stole it. I repeat, he is your enemy, and I will fight and kill him."

"Mowbray?" said the king.

"It is not true," said Mowbray between his teeth, "I have never planned to kill you, and I haven't stolen money from you. Name a day, your majesty, and I will fight and kill him."

King Richard looked at the two men. "Forget this. Be friends."

"I won't. I can't," said Bolingbroke.

"Never," said Mowbray.

The king said coldly, "A king does not ask. He commands."

Mowbray and Bolingbroke didn't answer.

"You must fight," said the king. "At Coventry, on September 17th, I will come to watch you."

At Coventry

So, in front of the king and queen and all the lords, Bolingbroke and Mowbray met to fight.

Music sounded. The two men lifted their swords, there was a breathless silence, and then, suddenly, the king moved his hand.

"Stop!"

Bolingbroke and Mowbray looked at him with surprise.

"Come here."

They went and stood in front of him.

"I have changed my mind," said Richard. "There will be no fight. I want peace in England, not blood and death. Bolingbroke, you will leave the country. You may not come back to England for ten years."

Bolingbroke bent his head. "You are my king,"

he said.

"Mowbray," said the king, "you too must leave this country."

"And when shall I return?"

"Never," said the king. "Never."

Mowbray's face was white. "This is too hard," he said. "I love my country. I've spoken English for forty years, and I'm too old to learn another language now."

"You must not argue with your king," said Richard.

"Then I will go into darkness," said Mowbray. "But first, Bolingbroke, I will say something to you." He spoke in a loud clear voice. "God knows you, Bolingbroke, and I know you. And soon, too soon, the king will find out what you really are."

Mowbray walked slowly away.

Old John of Gaunt looked at Bolingbroke with sad eyes, and the king saw this.

"Not ten years," he said. "Six, only six."

"The king speaks, and his power is great," said Bolingbroke, "four years disappear."

"Ten, six," said the old man. "I shall die before my son returns."

"Why, uncle," said the king, "you'll live for many years."

John of Gaunt shook his head. "No," he said.

"Say goodbye to your son," said the king coldly. "I have commanded, and he must go."

"You can't command me to live longer," said the old man sadly.

When John of Gaunt was alone with his son, he

tried to comfort him. "Only six years," he said. "Tell yourself it's a long holiday. Every place under the sun can be a home, if a man thinks rightly. If you can think you're happy, my dearest son, you will be happy."

"Impossible, father," said Bolingbroke.

"If I were young like you, I wouldn't stay here," said his father. "Come, I'll go to the ship with you."

Bushy, Bagot and Green

King Richard was a weak young man. He enjoyed his power, and he enjoyed acting like a king. But when he was with his three close friends, Bushy, Bagot and Green, he spoke quite differently.

"I'll tell you why I stopped the fight and sent them away," he said. "Men like them are dangerous. Bolingbroke wants my crown. And the people like him. I've heard him talking to them; so kind, so friendly. He's too popular."

"Well," said Green, "he's gone. Forget him. Now, my lord, we must think about other things."

"Ireland," said Bushy.

"Yes," said Bagot. "They're fighting against you, you'll have to send an army."

"I'll go there myself," said the king.

"But where will you get the money?" said Green.

"From the people," said Richard, "of course. I'll order new payments."

"Will they pay?" said Bagot. "They're already paying heavily."

"They must give me money," said Richard, "if I order them."

The Death of an Old Man

Old John of Gaunt was very weak. "Is the king coming?" he said to his brother, the Duke of York, "I must talk to him. He must change his life."

"He won't listen," said York, "he won't listen to anyone except those three, Bushy, Green and Bagot; and they agree that he should take the people's money and spend it."

John of Gaunt lifted a shaking hand. "I can see the future," he said. "England, my country, this jewel ringed by the silver sea, this beautiful land, is in fearful danger."

The king and queen arrived. The gentle queen kissed the old man. "How are you, dear uncle?" she said.

"Old, and ill, and unhappy," said the dying man. "But you are ill too, Richard. You don't rule your country well. You spend your time with bad friends, who only want to please you and help you spend money."

Richard was angry at once. "Old fool," he said, "how dare you speak to your king like that? I could tell my men to kill you."

The old man was too weak to say more. He was carried away, and York tried to quiet the king's anger. "He loves you, Richard," he said, "he loves you as much as he loves his son Bolingbroke."

"You must not say that name to me," said Richard.

One of the lords came in. "Sir," he said, "John of Gaunt is dead."

"I hope I'll die next," said York. "The dead can't feel sadness."

"He's dead and we're alive," said the king shortly. "Now, about the money for my war in Ireland. I'll take all Gaunt's money, his castle, his land, everything."

"Richard, Richard," said old York, "Gaunt's money belongs to his son. You can't steal it, you'll lose a thousand friends and make a thousand enemies. I dare not think what will happen."

"Think what you like," said Richard. The queen was crying. "Come my love," he said, "you mustn't be unhappy, you mustn't be sad. Tomorrow I'm going to Ireland, and I want to remember a smiling queen."

A Secret Plan

Three lords listened to York and Richard. They were Lord Northumberland, Lord Willoughby, and Lord Ross. They said nothing until they were alone, and then Lord Northumberland said, "Old John of Gaunt is dead."

"But his son Bolingbroke is alive," said Ross.

"But he has no home, no land, no money now," said Willoughby.

There was a long silence. Northumberland broke it. "The king is led by bad friends, and they hate us. If the king ordered them, they would take our castles and land too," he said.

"The people don't love him, he's lost everyone's

love," said Ross.

"And they have to pay him more every day," added Willoughby. "When will it end? I have no hope."

"I have," said Northumberland, "but I dare not say it."

"You can tell us," said Ross.

"All right, listen." He looked at the doors and windows, and lowered his voice. "I know that Bolingbroke is coming back to England with a large army. He'll wait until the king's in Ireland, and then he'll land at Ravenspur in the North, and march across the country. If you both want to join him, you can ride north with me and my son. If you're afraid, stay here, but keep our secret."

"We'll ride with you," said Willoughby and Ross at once.

Fearful News

The queen was sad and Bushy tried to comfort her.

"You must smile and be happy and please the king," he said.

"I'm afraid."

"Of what?"

"I don't know. Something bad is going to happen. I can feel it."

Green came in, white-faced and breathless. "Madam," he said, "Bushy, Bagot, has the king gone to Ireland?"

"Yes. Why?"

"Oh fearful news! Bolingbroke has landed with

an army in the north."

"Now I know why I am so heavy and sad," said the queen.

"And there is worse news, madam," said Green. "Northumberland and his son, young Harry Percy, and several other lords have ridden north to join him."

"And my uncle, the Duke of York?"

"He's here, madam."

The old man hurried in. "Uncle," said the queen, "say something to comfort me."

"I can't," said York. "I don't know what to do. Someone must go to Ireland and tell the king. And where can we get the money to fight these men? And how can I fight? Richard is my king, I ought to fight for him, but Bolingbroke is my brother's son and the king has wronged him deeply. Bushy, Bagot, Green, go and give orders to the soldiers. Madam, come with me."

He hurried away, shaking his white head, and the queen followed him. Bagot said, "We can't get an army together. Who would fight for Richard, or for us?" Green said, "I shall go to Bristol Castle. I have friends there. If I can reach them safely."

"I'll come with you," said Bushy. "Are you coming, Bagot?"

"I'll try to reach the king in Ireland."

He held out his hand. "We may never meet again. So this is goodbye."

"But not for ever," said Bushy, "not for ever. We may meet again?"

"I think not," said Green.

The Return

Bolingbroke and his army landed in the north. Old York came to speak to his nephew. Bolingbroke bent low. "My uncle York," he said.

"Don't call me uncle," said York angrily. "I'm not an uncle to my country's enemy. The king told you to leave England for six years. And now you dare to come back with an army. If you're looking for the king he is not here, and I am ruler of England while he is away. If I were young and strong, I'd fight you myself."

"I've done nothing wrong," said Bolingbroke. "When I left, I was the Earl of Hereford. Now I'm the Duke of Lancaster, which was my father's name. And the king has stolen everything."

"I know all that," said York. "I know the king has wronged you, but you can't come here with an army. That's not the way to put things right. You're an enemy to England."

"I've come for what is mine."

The old man shook his head. "I'm helpless, I have no soldiers, no power. Do what you like. I can't stop you."

The King Returns

The king sailed back from Ireland and landed on the west coast. Lord Aumerle, who was the Duke of York's son, and the Bishop of Carlisle were with him, and he had a few soldiers.

There was an old castle not far away. "What's that castle?" said Richard. "Berkley Castle, is it?"

"Yes, sir."

Richard stood still. "I'm crying and smiling," he said, "because I love my country. Let me touch the earth with my hand. Dear earth, do not help my enemies; let your stones become soldiers and fight for me."

"We mustn't waste time, your majesty," said Aumerle. The king wasn't listening. "When Bolingbroke sees me," he said, "he will shake with fear. God's king can never be destroyed; all the water in all the seas cannot wash God's mark from me. My army is God's army; and he will fight for me."

They heard a horse coming fast towards them. It stopped and the rider jumped off and hurried to the king.

"It's Lord Salisbury," said Aumerle. "A friend."

"Welcome," said Richard. "Where are your soldiers, Lord Salisbury?"

Salisbury bent his head. "Call back yesterday, tell time to return," he said. "Then you would have 12 000 fighting men. Today they've gone to join Bolingbroke."

Richard stared at him.

"My lord," said Aumerle quickly. "Remember who you are."

"Of course. I am the king. And I know my uncle York will have enough men."

Another rider appeared in a cloud of dust, stopped his horse, and ran to the king.

"Sir Stephen Scroop," said Aumerle.

"What is your news?" said Richard. "I'm listening, I'm not afraid."

"I'm glad," said Scroop, "because the news is very bad. Every man in England, it seems, young or old, has joined Bolingbroke."

At first the king couldn't speak. Then he said: "Bushy? Bagot? Green? Are they with Bolingbroke?"

"No, sir." He stopped. "They're . . . "

"They're dead? Are Bushy, Green and Bagot dead?"

"Comfort, sir," said Aumerle. "You must be brave."

"Don't talk about comfort," said Richard. "We'll sit on the ground and tell sad stories of the death of kings; and water shall fall from our eyes like rain upon the dusty earth."

"My lord," said the Bishop, "brave men don't sit and feel sorry for themselves. They help themselves. They fight."

"My father York has an army, surely," said Aumerle. "Sir Stephen, where is he?"

"Your father York has joined with Bolingbroke. All your castles in the north have fallen, and all your lords in the south will fight against you."

Berkley Castle

Bolingbroke marched successfully across England to the west coast, and camped near Berkley Castle. Northumberland's son, Harry Percy, was sent to the old castle to find out if anyone was

15

there. After some time, he came back.

"Welcome, Harry," said Bolingbroke, "won't these old walls receive us?"

"No, sir, because a king is there."

"What? King Richard is in the castle?"

"Yes, and with him Lord Aumerle and Lord Salisbury, Sir Stephen Scroop and the Bishop of Carlisle."

"My lord Northumberland," said Bolingbroke.

"Sir?"

"Go to the castle, sound the trumpets, and say you have words for the king. Tell him I won't fight. I'll send away my army, if he will let me stay in England, and give back what is mine. If not, this earth shall be red with the blood of Englishmen."

Lord Northumberland went. And Bolingbroke waited and watched. Suddenly he said, "Look up. Richard is there, on the walls, with Aumerle and the Bishop."

"He still looks like a king," said York.

There was a long silence. Richard looked down at Northumberland. Then he said, in a cold, clear voice, "I am surprised, Lord Northumberland. You should be bending low before me, your king. Why have you come?"

Northumberland told the king what Bolingbroke said.

The king turned to Aumerle and the Bishop. "What shall I say? Must I tell Bolingbroke that he is welcome, and shall have everything he wants? Or shall we fight?"

"No, my lord," said Aumerle gently, "We'll fight only with words, until we have more friends to help us. Tell Bolingbroke you agree."

Northumberland went back to Bolingbroke, and then returned.

"Well," said Richard, "what does great Bolingbroke reply? Shall I lose my name and my crown?"

"He is waiting below," said Northumberland. "He wants to speak to you himself."

"In that case I must go down to him," said the king, "down, down, down like a falling star."

Bolingbroke bent low before Richard.

"Stand up," said Richard.

"My lord," said Bolingbroke, "I've only come for what is mine."

"It's yours, and I am yours. What must I do now? Must I go with you to London?"

"Yes," said Bolingbroke.

In a Garden

In a garden outside London the queen was walking with her ladies. She said, "I wish I knew where Richard is, and what is happening."

An old gardener was working among the flowers and talking to one of his men. "These are fearful days," he said, "why didn't Richard look after his country as we look after this garden? He would still be king."

The queen was listening. "What did you say? Isn't Richard the king now?"

"No madam. Go to London, and you'll see. Bolingbroke has him. The king has no friends now."

"Is this really true?"

"Yes, madam."

17

"I'll go to London," she said, "and find my sad king."

"Poor queen," said the gardener when she went away. "I wish I could help her. Here, just here, she stood and cried; and here I'll plant a flower, and remember this most unhappy lady."

King Henry

In London, Bolingbroke sat in Parliament with his lords. York came to him.

"I've spoken to Richard."

"Yes?"

"He agrees. You shall be king."

"In the name of God, then," said Bolingbroke, "I will be king of England. But Richard must come here, everyone must see and hear him. No-one must say I stole the crown."

They waited. Then York came back with the king. Richard was really unhappy. But he knew that everyone was looking at him, he knew that the fall of a king was a fearful thing. He was like the most important actor in a play.

He walked slowly down the great hall to Bolingbroke. No-one moved or spoke; all eyes were on him. He began,

"You have brought me here too soon. In my thoughts I am still king." He looked at the lords. "I can see men who said they were my friends. They were not my friends. Bolingbroke, cousin, why have you brought me here?"

"You must say you are giving the crown to me." The golden crown, bright with jewels, was on a table in front of Bolingbroke.

"Give me the crown," said Richard.

York brought it to him.

"Here," said Richard, "take the crown. Take it. Now you are high and I am low. You can have my crown, but not my sadness. I am still the king of sadness."

"I shall be king of England. Do you agree?"

"Yes and no, yes and no," said Richard.

They waited.

"Yes," said Richard at last. "I hope your majesty will have a long life, and that I shall soon be dead."

Northumberland stood up. "Here is a list of your crimes. You must read it aloud."

"My eyes are wet, I can't see," said Richard.

"Read it."

"Leave it, Lord Northumberland," said Bolingbroke.

"Bring me a looking-glass," said Richard. "I want to see the face of a man who was a king, but now is nothing."

"Get a looking-glass," said Bolingbroke.

The looking-glass was brought. Richard looked at himself.

"Strange," he said, "this is the face of a young man, but I feel old."

He threw the mirror down and it broke.

"There, great king," said Richard. "Richard is broken in 100 pieces."

"Enough," said Bolingbroke. "When you give me the crown you give me all the cares and troubles of a king."

"But I still keep them," said Richard. "Now let

The looking-glass was brought. Richard looked at himself.

me go."

"Take him to the Tower of London," said Bolingbroke.

Afterwards Aumerle said to the Bishop of Carlisle, "A most unhappy play, with the saddest ending."

"It's not ended," said the Bishop, "your children's children and their children's children, will feel the fearful results of this bad day."

Goodbye

Richard's queen was waiting at the gates of the Tower.

"Look," she said softly, "here is the king, my love."

"Fair lady, dearest queen," said Richard gently, "don't cry, don't cry. We were asleep, we were dreaming, and now we're awake. You must go to France and stay there. We will meet in the next world, and wear our crowns again."

Northumberland arrived. "The king has changed his mind," he said shortly. "Richard, you must go to Pomfret Castle in the north, far away from London, and you madam must leave the country at once."

"Let him come to France with me," said the queen.

"What? And get an army there, and come back again and fight? Say goodbye, and be quick."

The End

Pomfret Castle was cold and dark. Richard was alone there; no-one came near him except the keeper who brought his food.

Bolingbroke knew that while Richard was alive, he was always in danger. He did not say, "Richard must die," but he did say, "Will no friend destroy this living fear?" and he was heard by a man called Sir Pierce of Exton, who wanted to please him.

Richard spent long lonely days, thinking and talking to himself. "This prison is my whole world," he said, "and like an actor, I must play all the parts." One day, he heard music. "A sign of love," he said, "a sign of love in a world that hates me." The music stopped and once more Richard's thoughts began to go round and round in his head. Then the door opened and a man came in.

"Who are you?" said Richard.

"You don't know me sir. I was the man that looked after your horses, sir, when you were king. I have tried to see you before but the soldiers wouldn't let me. I was very sad, my lord, when Bolingbroke rode your horse through the streets of London."

"He rode my horse? And he didn't fall?"

"No my lord."

The door opened again and the keeper came in with a plate of food.

"Out, you," he said to the man.

"You must go," said Richard gently. "You're

my last friend on earth. Don't forget me."

The man went. The keeper said, "Sir, will you eat your food?"

"Taste it first," said Richard.

"Sir, I dare not," said the keeper.

"Why not?"

"Someone has come from London, Sir Pierce of Exton. He told me not to taste the food."

Suddenly Richard was very angry. He jumped at the keeper, and the keeper shouted for help. Sir Pierce of Exton ran in with a sword. Richard seized the sword, but he was not strong enough. Exton hit him, and he fell. In a moment he was dead, his life was over.

Exton looked at the dead Richard. "You were brave," he said. "When you died, you were truly a king."

King Henry the Fourth

Cares and Troubles

"I wanted his death," said King Henry the Fourth when he heard that Richard the Second was dead. "But my heart is full of sadness. I'll go to Palestine, the Holy Land, and I'll ask God to wash this blood from my hands. When the land is quiet, I'll go."

A year later England seemed peaceful, and Henry said to his lords, "At last I can think about my journey to the land where Christ lived and died. Are the plans made?"

Lord Westmoreland answered him. "They are, my lord, but you can't leave England yet."

"Why not?"

"There is news of trouble in Wales. Lord Mortimer has been taken prisoner by the wild Welshman, Owen Glendower, and a thousand English soldiers are dead. And there is more trouble in Scotland," went on Westmoreland. "Young Harry Percy has been fighting, and he has taken several prisoners."

"Young Percy," said the king. "Don't they call him Hotspur? He's a brave fighter. I wish my son Prince Hal was like him."

"Hotspur has done well," said Westmoreland, "but he refuses to send his prisoners to you, as he should, so that the Scots can pay you to free them."

"Tell him he must come to London and explain himself," said King Henry. "His uncle, the Earl of Worcester, is no friend of mine, and he's taught young Hotspur to think he can do what he likes. Well, I see I can't go to Palestine yet."

Prince Hal

Prince Hal, the king's oldest son, was not interested in fighting. While his father waited for Hotspur, Prince Hal was drinking in the city with his friend Sir John Falstaff.

Sir John was very fat indeed. He was neither brave nor good, but he was amusing and Prince Hal liked to laugh at him.

"Where will you steal money tomorrow?" said the Prince.

Before Falstaff could answer, another of the Prince's followers arrived. His name was Poins.

"What news Poins?"

"Good news, boys," said Poins. "Tomorrow, tomorrow, boys, there are travellers coming to London with fat moneybags. I have masks for you, to hide your faces, and you all have horses."

"I'll come with you," said Falstaff. "Are you coming Hal?"

"What?" said the prince. "Me steal, me—a thief? I'll stay here."

"Then when you're king, I'll become an enemy of England," said Sir John.

"I don't care," said the prince.

"Sir John," said Poins, "leave me alone with the prince. I'll make him come."

Falstaff left the inn. "Now my dear sweet lord," said Poins, "ride with us tomorrow. I have a plan but I can't do it alone. Falstaff and the other three, Bardolph, Peto and Gadshill, shall attack the travellers. They'll take the money. And then, you and I will appear, and take the money from them."

"But won't they know us? Won't they be too many for us?"

"We'll tie up our horses in the woods, and I've got different clothes for us. And Falstaff, as you know, is more afraid of a fight than any man in England. It'll be a good joke, sweet prince. When we meet Falstaff afterwards, you'll see, he'll tell us he was attacked by a hundred men, and fought them all."

"All right. I'll go with you," said the prince.

Poins went, and the prince was alone. He said to himself, "I know you all, Falstaff, Poins and all of you. I'll go with you for a little while, but one day, when I'm king, I'll change. And then I'll shine like the sun after the clouds that covered it have gone."

Young Hotspur

There were very angry voices when Lord Worcester and Hotspur came to London and saw the king.

"I've been too easy with you, Worcester," said the king. "But now you'll find you have to fear me."

"Have you forgotten, sir," said Worcester, "the men who helped you to get the crown? Lord Northumberland, here, was one of them."

"Worcester," said the king angrily, "you may go. When I need you, I shall send for you."

Worcester went. "There's danger in his eye," thought Henry. "Now, Hotspur. You tell me you will give me all your prisoners, if I pay money to Owen Glendower, to free Lord Mortimer. But Mortimer is my enemy. He's married to Glendower's daughter. Well, he can die of hunger on the Welsh mountains. I won't pay one penny to save an enemy."

"Enemy?" shouted Hotspur. "Never. He fought Glendower and was wounded too."

"I don't want to hear his name again," said the king. "Send me your prisoners at once, or you'll hear something you won't like. Lord Northumberland, you may leave me, and take your son with you. I command you, send those prisoners."

The king went away, and Hotspur shouted after him, "I won't send them, you can cut my head off if you like but . . ."

"Hotspur," said his father, "wait — wait — think. Here's your uncle Worcester."

Hotspur wasn't listening. "I'll go to Mortimer and join him. Bolingbroke forgets who helped him win the crown."

"My son is very angry with the king," said Northumberland to Worcester with a smile.

"What's all this shouting about?" said his brother.

"Mortimer's my wife's brother," said Hotspur. "The king's afraid of Mortimer, that's what it is, the king's afraid."

"Peace, say no more," said Worcester. "I've something to tell you; something dangerous."

"I'm not afraid of anything," said Hotspur. "I'll fight . . ."

"Hotspur, will you listen to me?"

"I'm sorry sir," said Hotspur.

"You shall keep the Scots, your other prisoners," said Worcester.

"Indeed I will. The king told me not to speak of Mortimer. I'll go and shout 'Mortimer' in his ear. And then I'll . . ."

"Goodbye," said Worcester, "I'll talk to you when you're more ready to listen."

"When I remember," shouted Hotspur, "how I bent my head to Bolingbroke, at that place. What's it called . . ."

"Berkley Castle," said Northumberland.

27

"That's the place," said Hotspur. "Gentle cousin, he called me then, when he needed me."

"Have you finished?" said his father. "If not, we'll wait for you."

"I'll be quiet," said Hotspur.

"We have a plan," said Worcester. "Hotspur, you will return to Scotland, and get an army. The Archbishop of York will join you because his brother was killed by Bolingbroke. And then, we'll join with Mortimer, and the Welsh. And then . . ."

"Say no more," said Hotspur. "I understand. I hope we'll soon fight again, and bring this Henry Bolingbroke to the ground. It'll be a good day's sport."

News for Prince Hal

While Hotspur was planning war, the king's son was shouting with laughter in a London inn. He and Poins took the money which Falstaff and the rest stole from the travellers. Now they waited for Falstaff. At last the fat man arrived and called at once for a drink.

"Where have you been?" said Poins.

"I hate cowards," said Falstaff. "I hate men who won't fight. And you a king's son, a prince."

"What's the matter?" said the prince.

"Matter? You were too afraid to come. Where were you when we attacked the travellers?"

"Did you get the fat money-bags?"

"We did, and then fifty men attacked us and stole them."

"Fifty?" said Poins looking at the prince.

"Fifty and I killed half of them."

"Listen, you great hill of fat. Poins and I—just two of us—attacked you and took the money."

Falstaff shook with laughter. "I knew it, I knew it was you," he said easily. "But I couldn't kill the king's son, could I? That's why I ran away. And I'm glad you have the money, send for more drink."

"My lord the prince," said a voice. It was the woman who owned the inn. "There's a lord at the door sir, and he wants to speak to you. He says he comes from your father."

"Shall I talk to him?" said Falstaff.

"Please do," said the prince.

Falstaff soon came back. "Bad news," he said. "You must go to your father in the morning. Young Hotspur and—what's his name—Glendower, Owen Glendower, and Mortimer, and old Northumberland, and that Scotsman, Douglas—they're all against the king. Aren't you afraid?"

"No."

"Not even of Hotspur?"

"Hotspur, the man who kills sixty or seventy men before breakfast, washes his hands, and says to his wife, 'this is a lazy life, I need some more work'? No, I'm not afraid of him. But, boys, we must all go to the wars. I'll go to the king tomorrow, and Falstaff shall be a captain and lead his men into battle."

The King and his Son

"What have I done?" said the king to his son next morning. "Why does my son, who will be king after me, find his friends in the drinking houses, and never come near his father?"

"People tell you bad things about me, father. Perhaps they're not all true."

"King Richard wasted his time with bad friends. You are like him. Young Hotspur, the bravest of all fighters, is more like a prince than you are. And what will you answer, Hal, when I tell you that Northumberland and Hotspur, the Archbishop of York, Douglas the Scot and Mortimer have all turned against me? I suppose you'll join them."

"No, no, my lord," said the prince. "You mustn't think that, I'll never do that. I'll find Hotspur and fight and kill him; and then you'll know that I am your son. I promise you this, father. And I ask God to kill me, if I break the promise."

The king smiled at Hal, and said warmly, "You shall lead my army, Hal. Now I know you're my true son."

While they were talking a man arrived with fresh news.

"What is it?" said the king.

"Your majesty, your enemies are at Shrewsbury, and they have a great army."

At Shrewsbury

Hotspur was reading a letter, and as he read it his face grew longer and longer.

"Is your father coming soon?" said Douglas.

"He says he's ill. He's not coming."

"But we need him very badly now," said Worcester.

"What else does he say?"

"He writes that we should fight. He says we can't stop now, because the king certainly knows our plans."

"But is our army big enough?"

"Yes," said Hotspur. "And we mustn't lose hope. My father may be well soon, and if we're in trouble, surely he'll help us."

"But I wish he were not ill," said Worcester. "Our men will think, perhaps, that he's afraid. They'll believe that he thinks poorly of our chances."

"We'll win without his help," said Hotspur.

"Scots are not afraid of anything," said Douglas.

"But . . ." began Worcester,

"Here's more news," said Hotspur. "Sir Richard Vernon. Welcome, Sir Richard. What news?"

"My news will not be welcome," said Sir Richard. "The king himself is marching here with a large army; his youngest son Prince John is leading another, and Prince Hal . . ."

"What about Prince Hal?" said Hotspur. "He

won't fight; he sits and drinks and lets the world pass by him."

"Not now," said Sir Richard. "I saw him jump onto his battle-horse like the god of war himself."

"I'll ride my own horse and find and kill him," said Hotspur. "But I wish Glendower and the Welshmen were here."

"There is still more news," said Sir Richard. "Lord Worcester's soldiers will not be ready for two weeks."

The men were silent. Then Hotspur said, "The worst news yet."

No-one answered.

"How big is the king's army?" said Hotspur.

"Thirty thousand men," said Vernon.

Suddenly Hotspur laughed. "If it's forty thousand, I don't care. If we're going to die, we'll die bravely with a smile. When shall we attack? Tonight?"

"We can't," said Worcester.

"Why not?"

"We're not ready."

"Impossible," said Vernon. "We must wait for more soldiers. Can't you understand, sir? We can't possibly fight tonight." "Look," said Worcester. "Here's someone else from the king."

It was a man called Sir Walter Blunt. "I've come with an offer from the king," he said. "If you'll listen to me."

"Well?"

"The king wants to know why you're against him. If he has wronged you, he says you shall have everything you want, and he promises you will be safe."

"The king is very kind," said Hotspur, "but we have heard his promises before. Lord Mortimer is a prisoner in Wales. The king wouldn't pay money to the Welsh. So the Welsh would not let him go. I fought the Scots for the king and what did he do? He told my father and my uncle to go away."

"Shall I tell the king what you say?"

"No," said Hotspur, "my uncle Worcester will bring my answer in the morning."

Sir Walter Blunt went back to the king.

"This gives us another night," said Hotspur. "Tomorrow, if we fight, our soldiers and horses will be ready."

"You Owe God a Death"

"My Lord of Worcester," said the king when Worcester came to his camp in the morning. "You and I are old friends. We shouldn't meet like this. It's all wrong. We don't want war in England, we want peace. So must you fight?"

"I never wanted this war," said Worcester. "I'm an old man, I'd like to end my days in peace."

"So why . . . ?"

"When Richard was alive, my lord, you were our best and dearest friend. We helped you to get the crown. And then you forgot us."

"That's no reason for fighting."

Prince Hal said, "If we fight, Lord Worcester, hundreds of men will die. They need not. Tell Hotspur I will fight him myself; he and I will fight alone."

Worcester bent his head and left the king's camp. When he went Prince Hal said to his father, "Hotspur won't agree. He and Douglas are sure that they can fight the world, and win. We must be ready for a battle, sir."

Prince Hal went to find Falstaff. "Ready to fight?" he said.

"Prince Hal," said Falstaff, "promise me, if you see me on the ground in the battle, be a good friend: stand over me, and save my life."

"You're too fat," said Prince Hal. "Ask God to help you."

"Hal," said Falstaff, "I wish it were bed-time, and the battle over, and all of us safe."

"You owe God a death," said Prince Hal shortly.

"Maybe, but I don't want to pay him yet," said Falstaff.

The Battle

Prince Hal was right. "The king will never be our friend. Never believe it," said Worcester to Hotspur. "Prince Hal says he'll fight you—just you and he alone."

"And if I killed the prince?" said Hotspur. "No. Give orders for the battle."

The two armies moved to meet each other.

Hotspur and Douglas rode through their enemy's men, looking for the king. Falstaff didn't even try to be brave. "Give me life," he said to himself. "I'll save my life if I can. The soldiers I captained are nearly all dead, and those that are left will never work again."

Douglas at last found the king and fought him, but then Prince Hal arrived and Douglas was driven away.

"You saved me, Hal," said the king. "Now I must believe you. You don't want me to die."

"Never," said Prince Hal, "I never wanted you to die."

He turned his horse and rode away, and found Hotspur.

"You're the Prince of Wales," said Hotspur.

"And you are Harry Percy," called Prince Hal. "This world cannot contain both of us."

"The time has come," said Hotspur, "one of us must die." He rode his horse at Prince Hal. They fought, and while they were fighting, Falstaff arrived. He shouted brave words to Prince Hal, but didn't try to help him. Then Douglas attacked Falstaff from behind, and Falstaff fell on the ground. Douglas went to find another enemy, and Prince Hal at last forced Hotspur off his horse, and killed him with his sword.

He stood over the body. "Goodbye, brave heart," he said. "You were the best of all." Then he saw Falstaff's body. "You too? Poor John, goodbye to you. You'll be missed."

Prince Hal went to find his father, and Falstaff got up slowly. "What's this," he said, "Hotspur, dead? Really dead? I'll cut him with my sword, and make sure of him." He wounded the dead Hotspur.

"Now," he said, "come with me." He picked up the body.

"The time has come," said Hotspur, "one of us must die."

The prince was not far off. "I've killed Hotspur for you," Falstaff told him.

"I killed him myself," said Prince Hal.

"He wasn't dead. He got up again, like me, and I had to fight him; but I won. He's dead now."

"All right," said Hal, "you killed him. You can tell the king and then be rich and well loved."

It was late and the sun was going down over the battlefield. Above the shouts of the fighters, and the cries of badly hurt soldiers, he could hear the call for the end of battle. Prince Hal listened. "It's over," he said. "We've won. Now we must go and see which friends are living and which have died."

He had won the battle of Shrewsbury, but the king could not go to the Holy Land yet. In the north, Lord Northumberland heard about his son's death. Lord Morton, one of his friends, told him what had happened.

"And when Hotspur was dead," he said, "our soldiers ran from the battlefield. Worcester was taken, and now he's dead too."

"My son," said Northumberland.

"There is more news," said Morton, "the king has sent an army north, led by Prince John and Lord Westmoreland."

"Where is the king?"

"He and Prince Hal have marched to Wales; Mortimer and Glendower are still ready to fight."

"Heavy news," said Northumberland.

"But this is war," said Morton, "when men go to war, they know they may die. Now, my lord, the Archbishop of York has an army, and you know that men will follow him. They think he must be right. He talks about the dead King Richard, and tells them that the country is sick, and will never be well, until Bolingbroke is dead. We must make our plans."

Falstaff in Trouble

When he came back to London, Falstaff went to drink at his usual house. But there he found that the owner, Mistress Quickly, had sent for the Lord Chief Justice himself.

"What's the matter?" said the Lord Chief Justice. "Sir John Falstaff? What are you doing here? Did not the king send you north with Prince John?"

"Oh, great lord," said Mistress Quickly, before Falstaff could reply, "I sent for you to take him."

"Why?" said the Lord Chief Justice.

"For everything, my lord, everything, all I have," said Mistress Quickly.

"Sir John?" said the Chief Justice. "Must this poor lady send for me, to get her money back from you?"

"How much money?" Falstaff said.

"Don't you remember? You said you'd marry me, you said you'd make me Lady Falstaff? And then you kissed me, and asked me to bring you some money? And I gave it to you."

"The woman's not well," said Falstaff, "sick in the head."

"I know you, Sir John," said the Lord Chief Justice, "and I know how you use people like her.

Pay her, and say you're sorry."

"Come here, Mistress Quickly," said Falstaff. He said a few words in her ear. "I promise," he said.

"You said that before," said the poor woman.

"Only ten pounds," said Falstaff.

"In that case I must sell my silver drinking cups."

"Glass is best for drinking," said Falstaff.

"Well," she said, "I'll get the money. And you'll come to supper tonight? And pay me everything then?"

"I will."

"I've heard bad news," said the Lord Chief Justice, looking hard at Falstaff. "The king is ill."

Prince Hal returned from Wales and met his old friend Poins. But Hal had changed.

"I'm very tired," he said to Poins.

"Can a prince be tired?"

"I'm tired of my old drinking-friends, I don't like this kind of life any more. I know you all too well. A prince should not have such friends."

"Is it true, your father's ill?" said Poins.

"Poins, if I told you that I'm deeply sad, because my father's ill—would you believe me?"

"No, I don't think I would," said Poins. "You didn't like him, and you never went to see him."

"Yes," said Prince Hal, "no-one would believe me. Where is Falstaff, is he in London?"

"Yes," said Poins, "and at the same house."

"Shall we go and watch him? Put on old clothes, and let him think we're poor men?"

"We'll do it."

"Follow me," said the prince.

Falstaff was at supper with Mistress Quickly and her friends. But the prince did not stay long. A messenger came from the king.

"You are wanted, sir," he said.

"I'm wasting my time here," said the prince. He said shortly, "Falstaff, good night," and without looking at him, went out.

The Head that Wears the Crown

King Henry could not sleep. "Most of my countrymen are sleeping now," he said. "I am the king and I have music, and a bed, and a quiet room, but sleep won't come to me. Perhaps the head that wears the crown must always be uneasy." He walked up and down his room. "If men could know," he thought, "what their future will be, the happiest young man would sit down and die. It's not ten years since Northumberland was Richard's friend. And two years later, they were fighting. Eight years, only eight, since Northumberland was like a brother to me; worked for me, gave me all his love. And when Richard said to him once 'Northumberland, the time will come when you and Bolingbroke will be each other's enemies' he was right, Richard was right."

He stopped by the window and looked at the sky. "Is it morning yet? I'm ill, and that's why I have these sad thoughts. They say Glendower is dead, and the army I've sent to the north will surely win its battle. And when these wars are ended, oh when they're done, I'll go to Palestine, the Holy Land. Once, a fortune-teller told me, 'You'll die in Jerusalem.' I hope I'll go there soon.''

The Meeting at Gaultree

The two armies camped at Gaultree, north of the city of York. As usual, a lord was sent from the king's camp to the enemy. When Lord Westmoreland came, the Archbishop greeted him. "What have you to say? You are a man of the church, why are you fighting the king?" said the lord.

"Because I want peace," answered the Archbishop, "and we can never have that while Bolingbroke is king."

"It was better," said Westmoreland, "when the bells rang, and the people came to church to hear you."

The Archbishop did not answer. Westmoreland went on, "If you, my lord, will send your soldiers home, the king promises that you shall have everything you want. All wrongs will be put right. Agree to this, my lord, and let us be friends."

"I will," said the Archbishop.

He told his officers to pay the soldiers and send them away. Soon they could hear the shouts of happiness from the soldiers. Westmoreland sent his own men to tell Prince John that it was peace, not war.

One of the Archbishop's men returned, and said, "The soldiers are all going, sir, like schoolboys let out of school early."

"I'm glad to hear it," said Westmoreland.
"Now, my lord Archbishop, you and all your lords
are my prisoners. You are enemies of this
country."

"Is this right?" cried the Archbishop. "You
gave your promise."

"Were you right, to lead an army against the
king? No more words, my lord."

The Golden Crown

The king, still sick and weak, was asking about
Prince Hal. "Where is he now?" he said.

"In London, sir," said one of the lords.

"Who with?"

"With Poins sir, and his other followers, I'm
told."

"Oh my heart is heavy, heavy and sad," said
the king. "He hasn't changed. How can he be king
after me?"

His lords tried to comfort him. "Your majesty,"
said Lord Warwick, "the young prince only
studies these men. He's learning their language,
that's all. When he's king, he'll know his people
well."

Lord Westmoreland arrived with the news.
"Happiness your majesty, and better health. The
Archbishop and all of them are taken, and in
Wales, Owen Glendower is dead."

"I ought to be glad to hear this news," said the
king, "but — oh help me, I'm very ill, I can't see, I
can't move."

Very gently they took the king to his bed. "Put my crown here, at the head of my bed," he said.

When Prince Hal arrived, he said, "What's this? Wet eyes? How is the king?"

"Very ill. We should leave him and let him sleep."

"No," said Hal, "I'll stay and watch by his bed."

The prince saw the crown. Then in sudden fear, he bent over the king. "He's not breathing! Oh he is dead, and this crown has killed him. I'll take it away, I'll take your trouble, I'll keep it safe, and give it to my children as you have given it to me."

The prince went away very sadly. After a time his lords heard the king's voice, calling weakly.

"Why am I alone? Where is the crown?"

"Prince Hal was with you, sir."

"Prince Hal? Let me see him. No, he's not here. Did he take the crown? Couldn't he wait until I was dead? I was asleep, did he think I was dead? Bring him."

They brought Prince Hal.

"Leave me alone with him," said the king.

"Father, I thought I'd never hear you speak again," said the prince.

"You hoped you would not, Hal."

"No, father, no," said the prince. "I thought you were dead, and the crown seemed to be your enemy, and so I took it. I wasn't thinking about its power, or about being king, please believe me."

"God knows," said the king, "that I got this crown wrongly; and God knows, what cares and troubles it has brought me. But you will be a better king."

"I'll take this crown away, I'll keep it safe, and give it to my children as you have given it to me."

The prince's brothers and the lords arrived. The king's eyes were shut, and they waited in silence. Then the king said, "It's strange, my lords — but I think the room we were in, when you brought me the news of peace — I think it had a name. Can you tell me what it was?"

"Yes, my lord," said Warwick. "It's called Jerusalem."

The King is Dead, Let the New King Live Long

Falstaff and his friends heard the news. "You'll see," he said to his friends, "golden times have come. You shall all be lords, I promise. We must hurry to see him. Take any horse you like, we can break the laws now."

King Henry rode through the streets of London.

"Stand beside me, all of you," said Falstaff. "I'll smile as he passes, and you'll see, he'll stop and smile at me."

They heard the sound of crowds. "He's coming!" called Falstaff. "God be with you, Hal! Good Hal, sweet Hal, we are with you!"

"Speak to that man," said the king to the Lord Chief Justice.

"Get back," said the Lord Chief Justice to Falstaff. "How dare you crowd so near the king?"

"My king! My heart! It's me, your good friend!" called Falstaff.

"I don't know you, old man," said the king.

Falstaff stared at him, unbelieving.

"I'm not the man I was, not your friend. You

shall have money to live, but don't come near me. Keep away."

And King Henry the Fifth rode on, out of his past and into the future.

King Richard the Third

The Summer Sun

Many long years passed, and still the great lords of England fought each other, and still men remembered how Richard the Second died. King Henry the Fifth died, and his son, Henry the Sixth, died too. Now Edward the Fourth was king, and for a short time the country was peaceful.

King Edward had a brother, Richard, Duke of Gloucester. Peace did not suit this lord. He fought in the wars and killed many men. People knew, too, that he killed King Henry the Sixth, but no-one could prove it.

"The wars are over," Richard said, "dark winter has gone and my brother Edward shines like the summer sun. Our soldiers dance and sing and make love to the girls. But what about me? I'm short, and my back isn't straight, and even the dogs bark at me."

Richard smiled, an angry smile. "If I can't be happy, I'll be bad. I've already made some plans. I've told Edward about an old story; this story says that 'G' will murder Edward's children. I think he believes it. I hope he does. But I must straighten my face and hide my thoughts, because here's my brother George, the Duke of Clarence. And what's this? A soldier with him?"

Richard smiled at his brother. "Good morning, brother," he said, "where are you going?"

"To prison in the Tower of London," said George, "the king has ordered it."

"But why, dear brother, why?"

"Because my name is George."

"That's not a reason. You didn't choose your name."

George didn't answer.

"It's Queen Elizabeth," said Richard. "She hates us, and all the king's friends. We're not safe, George, we're not safe."

"No."

"Poor George," said Richard, kindly, "I am so very sorry. I'll talk to the king and you'll soon be free. Just wait."

"I have to," said the Duke. "I can't do anything else."

When George was taken away, Richard smiled again.

"I love you very much, dear brother. And so I'm sending you to God. You'll never come back. Now, I wonder if the king is feeling well?"

This question was answered almost at once. Lord Hastings, one of the king's men, told Richard.

"The king is ill," he said.

"Oh, that's very bad news," said Richard. "What do his doctors think?"

"They're afraid. They think he may die."

"Oh no," said Richard. "Don't say that. Where

47

is the king—in his bedroom? I'll go at once." To himself he said, "I hope he won't live. But he mustn't die yet. Dear George must be sent to God first. And after that, God can take the king, too, and then I'll be very busy indeed. I think I'll marry the Lady Anne."

Murderer !

Lady Anne was the wife of King Henry the Sixth's dead son. Richard killed her husband and his father in a battle. She loved them both, so it seemed impossible; she would not and could not marry Richard, the murderer. "But I'll try," said Richard.

He found Lady Anne and smiled at her.

"Murderer!" she said to him. "Murderer! Go back to hell, don't come near me."

"Sweet Lady," said Richard, "don't be so angry. It doesn't suit you. God says, we must return a good act for a bad one."

"You know nothing about God," she cried. "Worse than an animal! Get out of my sight!"

"Dearest lady," said Richard, "won't you let me tell you why I killed your husband? It was because of your beauty. Most beautiful lady, you are my sun, my life, I love you, I've always loved you."

"I don't believe you."

"Take my sword," said Richard. "If you hate me, kill me."

But Lady Anne couldn't take the sword.

"I want you to die," she said. "God knows I do,

but I can't do it."

"Tell me to kill myself, and I will do it."

She looked at him uncertainly.

"I wish I knew what you were really thinking," she said.

"I've told you. Look," he said, "take this ring, wear it on your finger. Let me put it on your finger. Believe me, Lady, I am truly sorry for my wrongs."

"Well," she said, "I'm glad you're sorry."

"And shall I come and see you again?"

"I will think about it."

Death in the Tower

When he was alone, Richard laughed. "She's mine! I killed her husband, that brave bright-haired young man. I murdered his father, and she knows it. But she takes my ring! Perhaps I've been wrong about myself. I must get a mirror, and look at myself again. I must buy new clothes. And I'll marry her. But," he added, "I won't keep her long. Her father Warwick was my enemy, and so . . ." He danced one or two steps; and then he thought, "George, my brother George. I told two men to come and talk to me about his death. Where are they?"

The two men were waiting.

"Are you ready?" said Richard.

"We are," said one.

"We need a letter from you," said the other. "We can't get into the Tower without it."

"Here," said Richard, "here's the letter. Now,

kill him quickly, do you understand. Don't let him talk to you."

"We're going to use our hands, and not our tongues," one said.

"I like you, boys," said Richard. "Go and kill him." George was sleeping when the murderers came into his room. He woke up in fear. "Who are you, why are you here?" he said. "To murder me?"

"Yes."

"What have I done? Who sent you?"

"The king."

"The king? Oh, then go to my brother Richard. He loves me. He'll give you money."

"Your brother Richard hates you."

"Oh no, no. He's good, kind and good."

"He sent us here."

"It can't be true. He said he'd help me."

"And he will. He'll help you to go to God. Look behind you my lord."

George turned his head, and the murderers jumped on him and killed him.

I Have no Enemies

"Now for the king," said Richard. The king was dying, and he called all his lords and asked them to say they would never fight each other again. The lords agreed to this, and the king lay back. "Now I've done a good day's work," he said. "But where is my brother Richard?"

"Here," said Richard, coming into the room.

"Richard," said the king, "we're all friends

50

here now. Hate has become love. Now I can die."

"I am glad, so very glad," said Richard. "And I hope that everyone here is my friend, too. I don't like to think I have an enemy. And I really think I have none."

"Our brother George isn't here," said the king. "Richard, ask him to come here."

"But," said Richard, "didn't you know? George is dead."

"Dead?" repeated the king. "But I sent orders to the Tower. I told them to free him."

"Oh my dear lord," said Richard, "your orders came too late. Don't be sad. He is with God."

I Can See the End

King Edward the Fourth was dead, and Elizabeth his queen was crying for him. Her friends tried to comfort her.

"Don't cry," they said. "God gave you Edward, and now God wants him again. Remember your little son, Edward, your little prince. He must come to London, and be crowned. His brother will be pleased."

The dead king had two young sons. The Prince of Wales lived in Ludlow Castle, in Shropshire. The other, the little Duke of York was with his mother, Queen Elizabeth.

Richard, too, was thinking about the little princes. He had one—not friend—but follower, a man who would do anything. This man was the Duke of Buckingham.

While the queen was talking about her young

sons, Buckingham said quietly to Richard, "I want to talk to you, sir, about a plan. The queen's family will be dangerous."

"Buckingham," said Richard, "you're my dear cousin, you think like me, you tell me what to do."

It seemed that the sky over England grew darker. People were afraid. The next king was a child, and the men around him were violent and dangerous. What would they do?

The queen waited for the Prince of Wales. Her other son, the little Duke of York was with her, and the Archbishop of Canterbury.

A man arrived.

"What news?" said the queen. "Is the Prince of Wales well?"

"The prince is well, madam."

"What is your news?"

"I am very sorry to tell you, madam, that three of your family are in prison at Pomfret."

"Who sent them there?"

"Richard of Gloucester and the Duke of Buckingham."

"What have they done?" asked the Archbishop.

"I don't know, madam," said the man.

"The tiger has seized the gentle deer," said the queen. "Now there will be blood and death and war. I can see the future, I can see the end."

She said to the little boy, "We'll both go to God's house, the church and stay there. We'll be safe there."

"I'll take you there," said the Archbishop, "and God will look after you."

I Don't Like the Tower

The little prince arrived from Ludlow.

"Welcome, sweet prince," said Buckingham.

"Welcome, dear cousin," said Richard. "You seem sad, are you tired? Was the journey hard?"

"No," said the little prince. "But I wish my uncles were here."

"They were dangerous men, they did not love you," said Richard.

"They never hurt me. I thought my mother would be here, and my brother. Where are they? Are they coming?"

"Here's someone who will tell you," said Richard. A man arrived.

"Where is my mother?" asked the prince.

"The queen, my lord, and your brother the Duke of York, have gone to Canterbury, to the church. The queen is afraid."

Buckingham said at once, "Afraid of what? Her son must come here. They need not hide."

He sent the man to the Archbishop of Canterbury.

"I hope my brother will come soon," said the prince. "Uncle Richard, when my brother comes, where shall we live, until I am crowned?"

"Your friends think you should stay at the Tower for one or two days."

"I don't like the Tower," said the prince.

"Your brother will be with you. What are you afraid of?"

"My uncle George died there."

"Afraid of a dead uncle? I'm your uncle too, and I'm alive. There's no need to be afraid."

"I hope not," said the prince, "but my heart is heavy."

Another Murder

"This Lord Hastings," said Buckingham to Richard when they were alone.

"Yes?"

"He loves the little prince and his brother. What shall we do?"

"Cut off his head," said Richard. "And, Buckingham, when I'm king, you shall have all the land and money you want."

The Lord Mayor of London

One by one, Richard, with Buckingham's help, killed all the lords who might refuse to let him be the next king.

"There's one more difficulty," said Buckingham. "The Lord Mayor, and the people of London. They must agree. How shall we do it?"

"Let me think," said Richard. "Now, if the Lord Mayor believed that the little boys were not really the children of the king and queen . . ."

"Then you could be their king. I'll go to the Mayor now. When I come back this afternoon, I'll have good news for you."

In the afternoon Buckingham came back to

Richard.

"Well? What did they say?"

"The people said nothing, not a word. I told them you were a good man, brave and gentle. And I said, 'All of you who love England, cry *Richard must be king*'."

"And did they?"

"They were like stones. Not one word."

"H'm. Is the Lord Mayor coming to see me?"

"Yes. Now, Richard," said Buckingham, "you must be an actor. When the Lord Mayor comes, he'll find you standing between two churchmen, with God's own book in your hand. And if the Lord Mayor asks you to be king, refuse. Refuse several times."

"I will," said Richard.

When the Lord Mayor arrived, Buckingham was waiting for him. "Welcome," said Buckingham. "I want to see the king, too, but I don't think he'll talk to us. Ah, here's my man now. May I talk to the Duke of Gloucester?"

"No, my lord," said the man. "He wants you to come tomorrow, or the next day. He's with his men of the church, and he can't talk about worldly things today."

"Go back," said Buckingham, "and tell him the Lord Mayor of London wishes to see him about important business." The man went.

"You see," said Buckingham, "that he's a good man, not like his brother, the dead king. England would be a happy land, if he were king. But I don't think he wants to be king. Oh look—there he is."

They saw Richard, walking slowly between two churchmen, with a big black book in his hands.

"Great Duke," said Buckingham, "let us talk to you. I know you are thinking only of God, but will you listen to us?"

Richard stood still. Then he smiled. "You must excuse me," he said, "my mind was with God. But what can I do for you?"

"Something that will please God," said Buckingham. "My Lord the Mayor here, and the people of London, want you to be king."

"Oh no, no," said Richard, "no. Impossible. The little Prince of Wales will be your new king."

"But, my lord," said Buckingham, "the little prince is not the next king. He can't be. He is King Edward's son, but the queen is not his mother. You must be king. You are the king's brother."

"Please, my good lord," said the Mayor.

"Don't refuse us," said Buckingham.

Richard said nothing, but turned the pages of his book.

"If you won't listen to us, we'll go away. But people will be very sad. Come, my Lord Mayor. The Duke is thinking about other things."

"Stop," said Richard in a gentle voice. "You're asking a lot. A king's life is full of cares and troubles. But I'm not made of stone. I will be king, if that is your wish, but the crown will be heavy, very heavy."

"God will help you," said the Lord Mayor.

A Rough Nurse

So Richard became King Richard the Third, and Lady Anne was queen.

"God knows," she said to Queen Elizabeth, "I don't want a crown. I let Richard talk to me with sweet words, and I married him. But since we were married, I've not had one happy day. He hates me, I know he does, because my father was his enemy. He'll kill me soon, I know he will."

"God must look after you," said Queen Elizabeth. "And I hope God will look after my little children. They're in the Tower and I'm not able to see them. The Tower, those cold grey stones—it's a rough nurse for my little gentle children."

Are You Made of Ice?

"I am king," said Richard to Buckingham. "But how long shall I be king? One day? Many years?"

"Many years, I hope," said Buckingham.

"Are you my friend, Buckingham? Are you really my friend?"

"Of course, my dearest lord."

"The Prince of Wales is still alive."

"True," said Buckingham.

"Buckingham, you weren't always slow. Don't you understand me? Then I'll say it clearly. The children in the Tower must die, and quickly. What is your answer?"

"You must do what you wish," said Buckingham coldly.

"Are you made of ice? Shall they die?"

"I can't answer now," said Buckingham. "Give me a little time." He went away. Richard was very angry. "Buckingham's afraid," he said. "I'll find

57

another way. I must. I must, I will, be safe. Who else must die? Anne, my wife. And then I'll marry the daughter of George, my dead brother. That's it. Then no-one can take my crown."

The Tiger and the Gentle Deer

He sent for a man called Tyrrel, a man who would do anything for money.

"Will you kill a friend for me?" said Richard. "Dare you?"

"Yes."

"There are two children in the Tower. While they're alive I can't sleep."

"I'll do it."

"Good," said Richard. "Very good, you shall have gold for it."

Buckingham came back. "My lord," he said to Richard, "I've thought about it—I mean those children in the Tower."

"You can forget it," said Richard. "The Earl of Richmond is in France."

"My lord, you promised me . . ."

"And some of the lords have gone to join him."

"My lord . . ."

"I remember now," said Richard. "King Henry the Sixth once said, 'The Earl of Richmond will be king. Richmond, the grandson of King Henry the Fifth'."

"My lord," said Buckingham, "will you listen to me?"

"There are two children in the Tower. While they're alive I can't sleep."

But Richard didn't seem to hear him. Buckingham went away. "I must leave England," he thought, "while I still have my head."

Tyrrel came to the king.

"Well, have you good news for me?"

"If the death of two children is good news, then yes."

"They're dead?"

"Yes."

"And their bodies are in the ground?"

"Yes."

"Come and see me after supper. And think. What shall I give you?"

"I'll think, my lord."

Winter Again

Richard walked restlessly up and down his room.

"The two princes are sleeping, and will never wake. Anne, my wife, has said 'goodnight' to the world. But still there's Richmond. There's the danger."

There were black clouds in the sky. War came near again, peace was gone like the summer sun. Buckingham was caught and killed. But the Earl of Richmond landed from France with an army, and was marching to London. Men from all over the country hurried to join him.

Richard led an army to meet him. Both armies camped at a place called Bosworth, in the centre of England.

Despair and Die

It was the night before the battle. Richard and Richmond were both asleep. It became very cold, and a shadowy ghost appeared. Richard saw it and was afraid. Richmond saw it and smiled in his sleep. It was Edward, husband of Lady Anne, killed by Richard. A voice said, "I will be with you when you fight tomorrow, Richard. Despair and die. But Richmond, I will fight for you."

The ghost was gone, but another took its place. It said, "I was King Henry the Sixth. You killed me, Richard and so, tomorrow you will despair and die. Sleep well tonight, Richmond," it said, "and live tomorrow."

Richard turned and shook with fear. He put his hands over his ears. But another ghost came and its cold voice said, "I'm George, your brother. Think of me tomorrow, Richard, despair and die."

"God is with you," it said to Richmond, "you shall live."

The ghost was gone, but now the air was filled with voices and moving shadows. The queen's family; Lord Hastings; Buckingham, all crowded round his bed. Anne his wife was there, and the ghosts of the two little princes. "Despair and die," they said to Richard. "We'll fight for you, and you shall live," they said to Richmond.

Next day the sky was dark over Bosworth Field. The battle began. It was soon over. Richard fought, and he searched the battle-ground for Richmond. When Richard's horse was killed, he fought on foot. He found Richmond, and Richmond killed him.

"The bloody dog is dead," said Richmond. "Now England can smile again, peace has come, peace lives again, and with God's help, will live here always."

"The bloody dog is dead."

Word Puzzles

A   Can You Read Quickly?

Example: On page 5 find the word which means 'a very bad
act'. Then read the whole sentence.

Answer: 'crime' 'Fighting against a king, or killing him, was
the worst crime.'

1   On page 6 find the word which means 'don't remember'.
2   On page 18 find the word which means 'a man who acts
     in stage plays'.
3   On page 28 find the word which means 'people who
     aren't brave'.
4   On page 47 find the word which means 'make straight'.
5   On page 37 find the word which means 'walked like
     soldiers'.
6   On page 8 find the word which means 'tried to help with
     kind words'.
7   On page 18 find the word which means 'put in the
     ground'.
8   On page 19 find the word which means 'a looking-glass'.
9   On page 8 find the word which means 'a time of rest from
     work'.
10   On page 24 find the word which means 'able to make
     people laugh'.
11   On page 28 find the word which means 'people who are
     journeying'.
12   On page 56 find the word which means 'not able to be
     done'.
13   On page 8 find the word which means 'liked by
     everyone'.
14   On page 35 find the word which means 'commanded'.
15   On page 61 find the word which means 'not easily seen'.

B   Right or Wrong?

Put R (right) or W (wrong) after these sentences.

Example: Shakespeare's King Richard the Third was a very
good man. (W)

1   King Richard the Second told Mowbray to leave
     England and never come back.

2 King Richard the Second died in the Tower of London.
3 Harry Percy was Bolingbroke's son.
4 Bolingbroke was sent away but he came back with an army.
5 King Henry the Fourth couldn't go to the Holy Land after he defeated Richard because there was trouble in Scotland and Wales.
6 King Henry the Fourth died in the city of Jerusalem.
7 When Bolingbroke's son became king, he gave Sir John Falstaff some money and a house.
8 George, Duke of Clarence, was Richard the Third's brother.
9 After Henry the Fifth died, Edward the Fourth became king at once.
10 The Prince of Wales and the Duke of York were the sons of King Richard the Third.
11 They were not murdered by Buckingham.
12 The ghosts told Richard the Third to 'despair and live'.
13 The Earl of Richmond was the grandson of Henry the Fifth.
14 Richard the Third planned to marry Warwick's daughter.
15 King Henry the Fifth was king before Richard the Second.

Answers

A 1 forget   2 actor   3 cowards
4 straighten   5 marched   6 comfort
7 plant   8 mirror   9 holiday
10 amusing   11 travellers   12 impossible
13 popular   14 captained   15 shadowy
B 1 R   2 W   3 W   4 R   5 R
6 W   7 W 8 W   9 W   10 W
11 R   12 W   13 R   14 R   15 W